Passport to the Future

Passport to the Future

Written by Barry Geistlinger

iUniverse, Inc.
New York Lincoln Shanghai

Passport to the Future

iUniverse books may be ordered through booksellers or by contacting:

iUniverse
2021 Pine Lake Road, Suite 100
Lincoln, NE 68512
www.iuniverse.com
1-800-Authors (1-800-288-4677)

ISBN: 0-595-34093-8

Printed in the United States of America

I never asked God to be the one to write a book full of revelations.

This book is dedicated to God our heavenly father. He helped me write it. He said he could only help me for three days because he had work to do. I think he's working on the ship made of light. It has to be big to carry all of us, and all the animals, and insects. I have felt God's love for a long time. Every time I speak in tongues he fills my body with love and energy. I recently began bowing to him to thank him for my girlfriend July. It was the only way I felt I could express my gratitude. I feel his emotions too, like he's showing me in person how he feels. I know his pain to give his only son to die for us. He missed his only son so much! I also know his pride for all of us. He's so proud of everyone for doing a good job keeping the Devil at bay. He has showed me that all life is good and that we should respect all the animals and insects. Even the plants that make the air good to breathe need respect. But the thing is, he can't kill the Devil without our help. He needs us to disarm him by showing love and compassion for one another. We need to recognize that the Devil feeds off our hate and he makes us doubt everything. He makes us doubt our selves, our loved ones, God, and all our dreams. So another way we disarm him is to laugh at him when he tries to discourage you. Tell him he's wasting his time trying to hurt you. You can also make it hard for him to get in your head by feeling love for any life. It can be love for God, your family, significant other, for animals, insects, or plants. The devil can't break through the love. All of this will disarm the Devil so God can banish him forever. The Devil will have no protection and won't be able to resurrect himself by us doing this. So that's all we have to do and God will be able to give us eternal life in the new world. We have fifty years to do this so let us not put it off.

Contents

FOREWORD

On December Third, Two Thousand Four, the same day I sent my first book "Love Profound" to the publisher, God showed me the future. I was speaking in tongues after my normal prayer where I was asking for my girlfriend July's protection. But this time it was different. As I was speaking in a strange language my mind knew what I was saying. I was feeling intense emotions and thoughts connected to the foreign words. I knew the world was coming to an end first, but I didn't know when. Then I knew God would be there to rescue us in a great ship made of light. Then I knew how the world would end, by a great meteor splitting it in two. I felt the loss of losing the world I knew and loved. But then I felt elated cause I knew we were going to a new world. And that July and me would somehow be populating it. At first I thought we would still have mortal bodies and that it was a new Garden of Eden with just her and I at first. But then I knew we would all have new bodies made out of light! These bodies could live forever and don't need food or air to live. And they could fly and go underwater and feel no pain. Then I knew how we would make love with the new bodies by merging with our soul mates and becoming one body. Then I knew a million souls with new bodies would pop out of her and I every time we made love. Then I asked about all the animals and insects and he told me they'd also be there to enjoy. Then he told me the universe is going to be our playground. Then he told me why the old earth was destroyed, in order to kill the devil inside. It all made sense. He told me the devil hid in the middle of the planet and it had to be split in two to destroy him. I started writing this book two days later. He told me it had to be finished in three days and I had to have it published right away. I didn't think I'd be writing another book so soon and in so little time. I wanted to wait for my first book to come out so I could get a big book contract and then write more books. So I'm paying to have this book published like my first one. God said he'd pay me back and I trust him without asking questions. If you read my first book, you know why I wrote it. It was all based on the inspiration I had from experiencing my girlfriend July's love from far away in Brazil. Just before I finished my first book we found out something incredible about ourselves. We could feel each other's thoughts and feelings deeply without any kind of contact, verbally or physically. Then we started getting the same ideas about ourselves at the exact same time without being in contact. We both understood that we are Adam and Eve reincarnated. God also showed her the future at the same time I was experiencing it. She hasn't told me what she saw yet, but she says she was everything. She has the power to see it; whereas, I have the power to know the details and the feelings associated with it. We still haven't met each other face to face. We only talk on the Internet and look at each other on our web cams. Basically this book is like a dream to me. My first book took three months to write and this one only took three days and God helped me do it.

EVERY DAY

Every day I miss my love.
Every hour my eyes I rub.

Every minute my heart goes out.
Every second I stumble about.

Missing you fills me with pain.
I am feeling so much strain.

I wish I could just go right now.
But I must wait for my book to come out.

Until then I will just keep writing.
It will keep my heart from crying.

To write is such good therapy.
My thoughts are clear for me to see.

I have to get out what I'm feeling.
Otherwise I will keep on repeating.

I must move on and keep going forward.
Otherwise I will get so bored.

I must write every Sunday.
Cause it is the most holy day.

That is when I'm most inspired.
Unto God I am hard wired.

He tells me things I can't imagine.
I am like his foreign legion.

I'll express just how I'm feeling.
His love for me has such meaning.

I can't explain how he makes me feel.
My body feels bigger and numb like a peel.

When I speak in tongues my body energizes.
Then there is knowledge my mind realizes.

I know how God felt to give us his son.
He missed him so much, cause he's the only one.
He didn't know if he would come back.
He could live forever and lay down some smack.

He would have to suffer up on the cross.
For us to be saved, cause our souls were lost.

He made the choice, whatever the cost.
He had no idea the pain was the most.

He cursed at his father cause he felt betrayed.
At his feet, the souls were laid.

Cause he made the ultimate sacrifice.
We were given life, not once but twice.

Now we are saved. Our future is awesome.
We are all like trees coming into blossom.

The life that we had doesn't compare.
There's a future that we all share.

We don't have the pain. We don't have the sorrow.
Our future holds unlimited tomorrows.

We take with us patience. We take with us virtues.
We leave behind all the things that can hurt us.

We'll be free of death, and free of worry.
There won't be a reason for us to hurry.

We don't have to think about work and money.
We'll have everything to make us feel sunny.

So reach in your heart and give out some love.
Don't be greedy if push comes to shove.

<u>ALL YOU KNOW IS LOVE</u>

God made you out of one of my bones.
He gave us a garden for us to call home.

In it we played with all of the animals.
There was no fear cause we weren't cannibals.

The birds, they landed, upon our fingers.
They sang such sweet songs. They were such good singers.

We rode on the backs of lions.
Our hearts were free of all evil signs.

We ran through the flowers completely naked.
We loved our naked bodies cause we weren't tainted.

The skies were so blue. It was like heaven.
There were no clocks striking eleven.

Time was on our side. We weren't under pressure.
The happiness there could not be measured.

We knew all the insects and all of the fishes.
We didn't make them into fine dishes.

Our love for life was self-evident.
We didn't quarrel or ever resent.

Our hearts were filled with God's great love.
He wrapped around us just like a glove.

We felt so protected and so immune.
How could we know it could end so soon?

You thought the snake was like all the rest.
But he represented more than a test.

He tricked you with all of his lies.
When you bit the apple it opened our eyes.

But what we saw was not at all good.
Our bodies we clothed, cause we felt we should.

The clouds became dark. Our happiness ended.
And for some reason, God was offended.
We felt so sorry we just ran and hid.
We had to think about what we did.

We were so ashamed. We were so nervous.
We thought, oh god, we don't deserve this.

But in our shame we still missed each other.
That is what brought us back together.

We had the will to find a way.
We brought our love closer together.

We had to make love while closing our eyes.
We could not look at what we despised.

A baby was born and we named him Abel.
We knew that new life needed a label.

His heart was pure. He made us so happy.
How did our next son turn out so crappy?

Because of the rain, our next son was Cain.
He cried so much from eyes that were plain.

We couldn't appease him, whatever we did.
His jealous heart couldn't be rid.

We tried to relax him. He wouldn't be calm.
He wouldn't listen to any psalms.

Everyone knows what happened next.
Cain killed Abel with no regrets.

The earth became an evil place.
You could tell by the looks on God's face

I CARE FOR YOU SO MUCH

My love for you cannot be compared,
to anything else in this world that's shared.

Just like love between God and his son.
Our love for each other can't be undone.

Miss you I do, when you're not there.
I know you miss me but don't be a scared.

Our future is set, already in stone.
God will make sure that we're not alone.

Together we are meant to be.
The future is ours for us to see.

We can see our love building and building.
We're like two volcanoes producing offspring.

Our love is so pure, that's why we were chosen.
To bring back life to those who are frozen.

The ones stuck between the old life and new one.
God gave his son to save us from ruin.

The future he changed so that we'd have meaning.
He shut out despair so we could keep greeting.

He's in our lives. We can't live without him.
He loves us so much because we are his kin.

His love is enormous. His passion is deep.
He is the master and we are his sheep.

He herds us around to where we are safe.
He works so hard every day.

He works because there's love in his heart.
It is for us even though we're apart.

We bicker and quarrel for no reason.
Cause the devil is guilty of treason.

He was cast out because he was jealous.
He wants to take God's love away from us.
He hid in the earth. He's right in the middle.
He's stuck like a thorn in our lives to meddle.

He is so evil. He is so bad.
He is the opposite of our dad.

He makes diseases. He makes bad thoughts.
We must leave so he can be caught.

God has a way to kill the Devil.
Cause he gives us so much trouble.

Once he is caught, evil will be gone.
Then it is time for us to move on.

We'll make our way to a new paradise.
It will be three times as nice.

There will be a sun bigger and brighter.
It will cast light and feel so much righter.

All the fishes will be in the sea.
We will not have to make them crispy.

We don't need food on the new planet.
Life will not be taken for granted.

The life will have worth and we will enjoy it.
It was so wrong for us to destroy it.

But do not worry. Our sins are forgiven.
God gave us all a shiny new ribbon.

He made us perfect, but we made a mistake.
Eve ate the apple and trusted the snake.

I AM BEARING A CROSS

I don't know when I'll get to be with you.
All I can do is try not to miss you.

I love you so much every day.
How much I love you is so hard to say.

Another minute passes and you're not there.
It is like getting kicked in the rear.

So much pain, cause you I am missing.
Being so far apart is really a big thing.

Inside we're so close, almost like one being.
Our thoughts are the same and so are our feelings.

God gave us a gift for us to share.
Our gift of great mystery will always be there.

He opened the cork and set our love free.
This kind of feeling gives me such glee.

Your love fills me up til I'm overflowing.
You see the future inside me I know.

God gave me great wisdom because I asked him.
He gave you great vision. Nothing gets past him.

He thought of everything so our future is bright.
We exchange our bodies for ones made of light.

We fly through the stars cause nothing can stop us.
He made us a playground that's straight above us.

We won't have to miss the animals, cause they will have a new home.
It's three times as big so that they can roam.

We will see great herds that move with a passion.
They will be free of any distractions.

There will be no pain. There will be no death.
Only happy thoughts will come from our breath.

The Devil is gone. His heart cut in two.
A meteor was sent to make him undo.
It will come in fifty years.
We don't have to worry, so don't shed the tears.

God is coming in a ship made of light.
He will rescue us and make the wrongs right.

We made some mistakes we shouldn't regret.
We'll have all the knowledge to keep us in check.

We'll know our past lives and be with our soul mates.
In love we'll combine becoming a floodgate.

Old souls will pop out of us making them new.
We're making a party for every two.

All soul mates will be together again.
They will make love again and again.

We'll all live forever, and speak the same language.
There won't be any hate for us to manage.

Til then we will live and have lots of babies.
Let us be careful so we don't get rabies.

We're going to make love on this planet.
It will be so good, I can't imagine.

Our love is so strong it will last forever.
God made sure we'd always be together.

There's no need for us to fear death. It doesn't exist.
The new world is ours filled with great bliss.

Inside it is love that we will pick up.
Our hearts will receive it and keep us warmed up.

WE'LL MAKE LOVE

We will make love amongst the stars,
in the rings of Saturn and even on Mars.

Our new light bodies will soon take flight.
We will have no reasons to fight.

When we make love, our bodies will merge.
It feels like the ocean when all the tides surge.

There will be no space between us.
Cause there will be one body between us.

When we combine it will feel like a dream.
Our thoughts will become one big flowing stream.

We will give birth to millions of souls.
Cause our love is completely whole.

We love each other more than this life.
There is such heartache. There is such strife.

It is too much for us to bear.
We are meant to love and to share.

This earth is a prison ruled by such evil.
Cause the warden is such a devil.

He is so bad, we can't imagine.
His heart is as cold as a haunted mansion.

His soul is as dark as an unlit tunnel.
His mind is as black as oil in a funnel.

He has no compassion. He only feels pain.
He threw his whole life straight down the drain.

We will be free from his devices.
We won't have to ask how much the price is.

<u>*RIDING ALONG*</u>

The sky is all blue. The clouds are all hiding.
I'm holding on tight to this horse we're riding.

It lowers its head and picks up great speed.
It's moving along like a thoro bread stead.

It's hooves beat the sand in a rhythmic pattern.
It's mane whips about like a storm on Saturn.

It's breathing so hard exerting itself.
It is a vision of perfect health.

Its coat is so shiny and a little sweaty.
It isn't tired cause it's always ready.

We're feeling the wind blowing past our faces.
We are visiting all foreign places.

We leave behind a past that is shattered.
Our hearts could move on cause they knew what mattered.

Our hearts are beating always together.
Our souls will be one forever and ever.

Our lives have been changed. We smile at the future.
We have become one with nature.

No longer are we requiring sustenance.
Life in the new world can live in abundance.

Our chains will be broke free from this earth.
We will be given a second birth.

To receive a new life how it was meant to be.
We were always meant to feel like we're free.

The freedom was lost, cause we didn't listen.
We made a mistake while doing his mission.

We screwed up so bad we lost everything.
It's not our fault what the devil brings.

God had nothing to do with our failure.
His love is something we should all treasure.
He is there trying to give us love.
We just have to ask for it from above.

Those who ask him, they will receive.
Just have faith in what you believe.

There is no one to blame when we defeat ourself.
So don't blame someone else. Only blame yourself.

The wealth of the heavens is there for the taking.
You have to bring out the love that you're making.

Life goes on. It won't wait for anyone.
So don't waste your time acting like some heroin.

The virtual world is such a big waste.
It is not even a real place.

I have played games like Everquest.
All that it did was put me in debt.

WITHOUT A DOUBT

You can doubt what I say. It's your prerogative.
What purpose does it serve to be so negative?

I have felt great sadness. It was how God felt.
Giving his son was not for his health.

I felt such great loss, as the earth was destroyed.
It felt so bad to lose what I enjoyed.

I felt such great surprise to see the great ship.
It was huge, made of light within grip.

I felt the relief to receive a new body.
One made of light didn't feel gaudy.

I felt the joy to see the new world.
Its beauty approached us and was unfurled.

I felt so happy knowing we could still make love.
Plus it is more special than the old way to love.

It felt so good knowing we will all live-forever.
The new life we have is so much better.

I was overjoyed to know there would be animals.
To not look at them like they were edible.

It was a joy to know we could fly.
Our bodies can now be one with the sky.

It felt terrific to swim with the fishes.
Not having to breathe air from the surface.

Just know that life is going to be saved.
And will not end in a shallow grave.

PERFECT IN EVERY WAY

How can I describe that which is perfect?
Maybe I'll start with your wonderful respect.

You cherish all life on this earth.
Without your love I'd lose my self-worth.

You are also giving and sweet.
You give your love like it's a treat.

And in your heart there lives a love.
That blows away any that other girls give.

You were born with such integrity.
I can trust you to run the economy.

How do you express so much sincerity?
The things that you say cast out disparity.

I wish you didn't have to work so much.
For all the time you spend, your expenses aren't touched.

Don't get me started on your beauty.
That would make this book sound really fruity.

The thing that's important is your devotion.
There's no way you'd leave me unless you're under some potion.

Nothing's more perfect than your innocent shyness.
The lights must be out for you to undress.

But I can see what goes on in your imagination.
You think of us on every occasion.

I FOUND MY SOUL MATE

I found my soul mate. Yes it is true.
Her eyes are green and she likes to wear blue.

Her skin is soft, and lips are supple.
I beg a kiss, if it's no trouble?

You're full of style. You look like a model.
You are so sexy that I cannot dottle.

I knew from day one we were meant to be.
You already had made me feel happy.

You accepted my compliments like they were golden.
Like I was someone who deserved more attention.

Our hearts fit together like two missing pieces.
It feels so good that I must repeat this.

Just like two magnets our hearts became one.
They won't pull apart cause the force is too strong.

There is a bond that holds us together.
One made from love and discipline forever.

The devil cannot corrupt our souls.
We're out of his reach, cause our spirits soar.

We were together at the dawn of time.
I'll always be yours. You'll always be mine.

We shall not part. Not for one second.
I could never be sick of your love so come get it.

INFINITE FAITH

Just ask God for infinite faith.
And your heart will not doubt the love that you make.

He'll cast aside any doubts that you have.
Clearing a path for you to feel glad.

Melting away all past transgressions.
Helping you turn mistakes into lessons.

It feels so good to be free of worries.
It's a thorn in your side that makes your thoughts scary.

You have to kick out any bad thoughts.
Like an unwanted guest you tell to get out.

Those thoughts don't have purpose. They're just there to scare you,
away from a dream that could repair you.

It doesn't make sense for your mind to battle.
It needs a direction for it to rattle.

You'll get everything done without those distractions.
The will of your intent breeds the result of your actions.

There's a time to chill and to just go with it.
Your mind is relieved to know you're one with it.

The Devil projects those doubts into you.
He wants to see you fail and point his finger at you.

He gets a kick out of seeing you discouraged.
He wants to take away all of your courage.

WASTING HIS TIME

Let's turn and point the finger in the other direction.
Tell the Devil he's wasting his time with those distractions.

You've got the knowledge to know what he's after.
So call him on it with all of your laughter.

Make him regret the time that he's wasting.
Fooling around like someone wine tasting.

He's spinning his wheels trying to hurt you.
You have God's love to never desert you.

His heart is bigger than a hundred-story building.
And you don't have to take an elevator to reach him.

He cracks his neck and the whole universe shakes.
When he flexes his muscles the space-time continuum breaks.

He's willing to give you everything you want.
Whatever it is, just send a shout out.

You don't have to doubt that he cannot give it.
Whatever you want will be on exhibit.

A house, a boat, or maybe an airplane.
Whatever you say to him won't sound insane.

A car, some money, or even world peace.
All of his love is there to release.

The future, it holds for us a new master.
One who loves us just like a bastard.

HAPPY AND LAUGHING

The lord, he wants us just to be happy.
There is nothing about him that's crafty.

His heart is pure just like two hundred proof.
The strength of his love could go through the roof.

You're building him up by asking for things.
The size of his strength comes from your heart rings.

You can energize the more that you listen.
For a message he brings for you to be forgiven.

He would not of done it if we didn't matter.
Inside of his heart is goes pitter-patter.

It's OK to cry if you're feeling joy.
You are grown up now. You're not girls and boys.

The joy that I'm after comes from inside.
It's there for a reason that you cannot hide.

The more you suppress it, the more it cries out.
It needs some attention to bring the light out.

Your heart tends to glow. I bet you don't know.
It glows like a sun wherever you go.

You could be in the ocean. You could be underground.
You could be in the worst part of your town.

You could be in the back of some stranger's van.
And God will come running as fast as he can.

THREE FAITHS

Number one is to believe in your self.
Put your faith in number one.

Put your trust in your inner voice.
It only wants to make the right choice.

Don't deny what you're feeling.
Worries and doubts do not need spreading.

Don't think that you don't deserve happiness.
A smile on your face will not come from success.

Number two is to trust in God.
Give him your love with a wink and a nod.

Show him your love and he won't reject it.
He knows the way to make you perfected.

Keep your heart stoked. Don't let it go out.
His love will be there. You can't put it out.

Keep your eyes open to thoughts that have feelings.
You won't have to worry unless you are stealing.

Number three is to trust your soul mate.
They were made for you to propagate.

Without them the enemy would have free reign.
The where and the why could drive you insane.

They were always included in the master plan.
So go find yours as fast as you can.

I GOT YOUR BACK

I'm right behind you righteous dude.
You always knew we'd turn out good.

You never doubted we would overcome,
the slings and the arrows from the terror some.

You gave us your son. I knew it was hard.
But he came back to your backyard.

You bent over backwards. Did anything for us.
You proved you were worthy by how you adored us.

You answered our prayers and forgave our trespasses.
You mended our hearts from all of the represses.

You guided our thoughts and shifted our vision.
You helped us make all the right decisions.

You guided July and I together.
You gave us a life that lasts forever.

You opened up the door to the future.
Our link to the past is becoming looser.

You gave us bodies that always make love.
We will find out with a sign from above.

You gave us a way for us to get out.
The ship made of light is moving about.

You are here to take us far away,
to a better place where everyone can stay.

ORIGINAL BEST

The soul mate you gave me is the best one ever.
Her words are soft just like a feather.

Her heart is good. She will never lie.
She thinks that I am the best guy.

Her love for me is incredibly great.
She has a look I cannot escape.

She makes me feel special with all of her words.
I used to feel like such a turd.

She doesn't give me trouble. Her will is to help.
She's so lovable I do not need wealth.

Her love is so deep. For me it cries out.
When will we be together? I want to find out.

I miss her so much, inside me I'm crying.
I will not cheat on her. There is no use trying.

We're meant to be together for the rest of time.
I love her so, because she's so fine.

She is lovely outside and inside.
Every time we talk it is verified.

She never gets tired of saying she loves me.
She cannot hold back the love she makes for me.

Together there's nothing that we can't do.
Our love can make the skies much more blue.

INSPIRATION IN SILENCE

Turn off the TV. Turn off the music.
You have a gift from God, so use it.

Put all your thoughts onto some paper.
Let God guide you to life that's forever.

He'll give you the words to make some ideas.
He will deliver a great panacea.

He has the cure to every disease.
Even the ones that make you sneeze.

He has the power to wipe out all evil.
Look in your heart and you'll know it's real.

You don't have to take no for an answer.
There is no reason for you to fear cancer.

Everything that was uncurable.
Soon will be gone freeing our souls.

The life that you had was ruled by a devil.
He hid in the earth causing such trouble.

He hates us so much he's gritting his teeth.
He's scheming about from the beneath.

We all have the power to cast him away.
Cause there is hope for a brighter day.

God put the future out on the table.
It's clear for us now to be free of labels.

WE THOUGHT

We thought every one was so different.
We didn't know God was giving a present.

There's a new way to live and be free.
We can enjoy the fish in the sea.

We can take a fantastic voyage.
Without needing a ship for storage.

We'll be self-sufficient. Need things we won't.
You don't have to take things with you, so don't.

When we board the ship we just need ourselves.
So just walk towards it leaving things on the shelves.

All your possessions and your belongings.
You don't need things you've been longing.

Money won't be useful up there.
Your new bodies will free you from your cares.

Money and power are completely useless.
You don't need a thing to fly through the blueness.

God has taken care of everything.
You won't even need water from a stream.

You won't need to breathe. You won't need to eat.
You won't need to drive a car on the street.

You won't need a house for you to live in.
God is giving us an earthly heaven.

I PROMISE

I promise to do what God tells me.
I do not ask why I'm so happy.

The tears that I cry are because of joy.
There is a reason I was deployed.

The time has come for us to unite.
Cause the Devil will put up a fight.

He doesn't want to give up what he's got.
He is so selfish and we are not.

We will prove to him that love conquers all.
All of our love will make him fall.

Falling from power is what he needs.
The hate makes him strong. On it he feeds.

We don't have to give him any more.
We know what God has in store.

His master plan will come to fruition.
He will redeem us cause it is his mission.

In our lives, he's always been there.
Giving us strength to release our cares.

With him by our side we become a force.
To destroy the Devil filled with remorse.

Make the Devil feel so guilty.
Tell him that he's incredibly filthy.

OH THE PAIN

Make the Devil feel nothing but pain,
for trying to make our lives so insane.

When he sees the love, he will start to suffer.
We will make his job a whole lot tougher.

Your love can be like a thrown dagger.
Piercing his heart. Making him stagger.

We can bring him down and cause him grief.
We just have to be strong in belief.

Without our hate he will start to worry.
He won't know what to do to make our lives blurry.

He'll be like a laser stripped of its power.
Just there waiting for the final hour.

He'll be so confused he won't have a clue.
He will just know that he is screwed.

Just like some prey attacked by a lion.
His eyes will look scared and he will start crying.

God will sink his claws into his skin.
Ripping him apart just like he was sin.

There will be nothing left when the battle is over.
The Devil will poof and be gone forever.

Then we can move on and be free.
The new world is the place to be.

Barry Geistlinger

I'M WAITING AND WANTING

The time will not listen to me to move faster.
I have to do the will of my master.

I wish I could just leave and come get you.
I was not meant just to impress you.

We were made for each other.
I bet you get your looks from your mother.

Your eyes are like a peaceful abyss.
It looks like your lips were made just to kiss.

I love your nose. It looks good to smell.
I love your hair. I bet you can tell.

Your chin is special. It frames your face.
I know that your tongue has terrific taste.

You have such nice shoulders for me to kiss.
When we make love, we'll only stop to piss.

Your arms are so delicate and so are your fingers.
You could hold a MIC and look like a singer.

You have such a tiny waist.
Between your legs there is such a space.

How does your butt start up so high?
It blends right into your thighs.

You have such nice legs and nice little ankles.
Your body was made with all the right angles.

I'M REUNITED WITH EVE

Our love began in the garden.
Unto me, you would harken.

I would come running, hearing your call.
I had a love for you most of all.

It is back with me. I'll never forget.
I will look back and never regret.

The decisions we made. The lives we led.
I will reflect as I lay in bed.

The silence, it puts my mind at peace.
So I can look back even through a crease.

My heart became full when I found your love.
We are paired for life like we are two doves.

We don't want to leave each other alone.
I stare at your picture when I am home.

Your love is giving me so much strength.
I will never doubt you. Your love will not sink.

Your love is like a buoy floating on the water.
It is held buoyant with love from the father.

You never questioned if my love was true.
You put all your faith in one that you knew.

You knew I was good. You knew I had feelings.
You knew I had a heart that is worth stealing.

I SHOW HER, CAUSE I KNOW HER

I know you are genuine. You never lie.
Your life is in balance, though time has gone by.

You don't have to give up any of your morals.
Your heart is like a basket of florals.

I can smell your love and devotion.
It fills my nose like air from the ocean.

It is filled with mist and deionized.
There is no smoke to be a disguise.

The smell is so pure. Your love is so innocent.
There is no doubt that it is heaven-sent.

God gave you more than anyone else.
He made you perfect unto himself.

He put a piece of himself inside you.
He knew there would be only one to have you.

I am that person. He made me so lucky.
All of my friends know me as Bucky.

They are the best friends anyone could have.
They are so good, I never feel sad.

I trust them all. I know they know better.
They don't forget me in the stormy weather.

They don't just call me when things are good.
They bring me presents and bring up my mood.

OBSESSION

Don't be obsessed with things you don't have.
You have the best love from a good dad.

You don't have to settle for the one here on earth.
He didn't have much to do with your birth.

He didn't have to carry you in his womb.
He didn't have to push you out of that tomb.

He didn't have to nurse you, when you were young.
He only had to call you his daughter or son.

You don't have to dwell on his misgivings.
He did what he could to keep you living.

It wasn't his fault he felt disconnected.
He wasn't as close as your mother protected.

His job was different than your mother's.
He had to support you and your brothers.

He had to work hard every day.
He made a sacrifice while he was away.

He gave you a love that you can remember.
He paid for the gifts you got in December.

He had to provide all the materials.
To keep you fed, stocked up with cereals.

Because he worked hard, he had to get free.
And be with his buddies. I hope you can see.

Barry Geistlinger

LIFE IS NOT HARD

Life isn't meant for you to be guessing.
Why you are here, or why you are stressing.

We're here to learn how to love.
He gave us an area to become a club.

The love will flow forever between us.
Keeping us warm like the air on Venus.

The love we give out will always come back.
In some other form you don't have to track.

When you help someone, you benefit more.
Your body feels good. Your spirit will soar.

It doesn't take much to do a good deed.
Just find somebody who is in need.

You can figure out what they are missing.
Maybe some change, or maybe some listening.

With all of the wealth that people are hoarding.
It takes just a fraction for charities supporting.

The ones filled with hunger and bad disease.
They need food and medicine and they say please.

It's not like they're asking for you to give up.
All of the things that keep you warmed up.

So don't be a greedy stingy old scrooge.
Give with your heart. It takes away blues.

<u>NO, YOU ARE</u>

You are so sexy.
No, you are.

You are a babe.
No, you are.

You are perfect.
No, you are.

You are incredible.
No, you are.

You are the best.
No, you are.

You are so loving.
No, you are.

You are a genius.
No, you are.

You are a fox.
No, you are.

You are so pretty.
No, you are.

You are so special.
No, you are.

You are like a model.
No, you are.

Barry Geistlinger

LOVE FROM THE SUN

Make sure you enjoy the sun when it's out.
It radiates heat so you can get out.

It gives your skin color so you don't look pale.
You don't have to wait for it to go on sale.

It gives you the vitamins your body needs.
So why don't you just roll up your sleeves?

You can go for a walk or maybe a stroll.
The light from the sun won't be undersold.

It is nice and yellow. No, it's not harsh.
If it were white, the life it would starch.

It is the perfect temperature for you to enjoy.
The air isn't just for breathing, no doy.

The air filters out the harmful rays.
And holds just enough warmth from every day.

The earth is performing a balancing act.
The plants and animals you shouldn't subtract.

The plants make the air able to breathe.
The animals return life to the seeds.

We should take good care of all of them.
We shouldn't destroy any of them.

Even the weeds are there for a purpose.
Their seeds spread more easily in order to help us.

I'M WHAT YOU'RE CRAVING

You want a man who's big and strong.
In my arms is where you belong.

You want a face that's like an angel.
You tell me that I should be a model.

You want a man with a hairy chest.
Deep in your heart, you know I'm the best.

You want to rub your hands on my muscles.
We are so different the leaves will rustle.

You know that I am good at dancing.
You cannot wait to start our romancing.

You want a love that lasts forever.
I will hug you tight like a sweater.

You want a man whose feelings are true.
You give me love to know what to do.

You want me more than anything else.
You are not interested in wealth.

You are constantly thinking of me.
You trip and fall, because you love me.

Your arm and your leg were practically broken.
Cause you were walking with you love wide open.

I want to take away your distractions.
When we are together, our love will take action.

Barry Geistlinger

HE BELIEVES IN ME

He knows that I can do the job.
He knows that I am not a slob.

He speaks to me and I hear him.
I feel every word like we're in rhythm.

He and I, we are a team.
He is making life a dream.

I trust in him. His vision is clear.
He just wants to take away all our fear.

He's breaking us free so we can enjoy life.
He gave us the best partners to share life.

We had to find out, one way or another.
That life is forever we got from our mother.

With him we are safe from evil and torment.
He is watching out for our government.

He's shifting the tides so we can be as one.
The world will have peace because of his son.

Our slate is wiped clean. There's nothing to burden.
Our souls will be free just like we're in heaven.

We'll stay in this plane enjoying the stars.
Our hearts will be free to go very far.

We have found out what he has in store.
We don't have to stay on earth anymore.

I HAVE FAITH IN GOD

I always knew that you loved me.
You love is bigger than any I see.

You care so much for all of your children.
You won't let us down. Your love will rebuild them.

You're back from a mission to make our lives better.
You left nothing out. Not even the weather.

You give us the trees so we can see beauty,
on a new earth. You made it your duty.

You worked so hard because you love us.
If you were here, you'd definitely hug us.

I feel your love. It couldn't be more pure.
You'll remove all disease and give us the cure.

Inside you, there beats a heart made of light.
It radiates love even when it's night.

It shines like a beacon for us to follow.
It gives us a future that we can swallow.

There is no hate inside you. You do not place blame.
The love that you give us is always the same.

It's not like a faucet turning on and off.
It's more like a cannon always going off.

You now have the Devil clear in your sites.
You're going to hit him with all of your mite.

THE CLOCK IS TICKING

Time is counting down on that little demon.
He's shaking so much inside he is screaming.

God is going to remove that which is evil.
You don't have to ask yourself if it's real.

He's waiting for the perfect moment.
When we are all ready to understand romance.

He wants us to show the Devil how strong.
Our love can be a heavenly song.

We can make the Devil's life a real bitch.
If we trust in ourselves, he'll start to twitch.

He will become weaker than he was ever.
He will gain strength if we don't stick together.

God needs our help if we're going to do this.
He needs all of us to make this a success.

In his weakened state he won't have protection.
We have to blank out feelings of rejection.

We need to have faith in God and his power,
in every minute of every hour.

Together we have the power to eradicate,
a Devil whose heart will not associate.

Banishing him has become our purpose.
We are God's troops controlling the surface.

THE HOUR HAS COME

The hour has come for us to be steadfast.
Forget all the worries you had in the past.

You can be stronger than ever before.
God is opening up the door.

The door to the future. The door to his power.
The door to the heavens. The door to forever.

He's ready to bless you more than ever before.
The new world is finished ready to explore.

He had to work hard filling it with love.
So there won't be room for evil to shove.

He's coming here now. He's making the journey.
Only he knows when it won't be early.

Let's make the most of these fifty years.
Let's all help each other erase all the tears.

We have no reason to be greedy.
The new life we have will not make us needy.

We won't have a care. We're all taken care of.
A body of light does not need a sheriff.

Our hearts will be free of all doubts and worries.
Clearing the way for our love to flourish.

Our hearts will be paired unto our soul mates'.
We're free to make love without any rebates.

Barry Geistlinger

SHARING EACH OTHER

It will be easy to share of our selves.
We don't have to focus so much on our health.

When we're made of light our needs are all met.
The past will be there for us to forget.

All that once was will be destroyed.
The houses and cars won't need to be enjoyed.

You won't have use of material things.
Your life will be free of all those bell rings.

You don't have to work. You don't have to slave.
There's no need for money. You won't need a grave.

Our hearts will be free to love one another.
It will be so good you cannot do better.

You don't have to beat your life to a drum.
We all can slow down and be more like chums.

We can value each other for our inner beauty.
And worship a lord who thinks we're all cuties.

We are his babies, every one of us.
It's in his heart to give divine to us.

You just have to ask and you shall receive.
He can only give to you if you believe.

So don't bring your self down if something bad happens.
You have the power to unlock the heavens.

THE FINAL SHOWDOWN

When the comet comes the devil will be helpless.
He won't have the power to even affect us.

He'll be like a tree stripped of its bark.
He will fall down with just one spark.

He won't even have a leg to stand on.
He will be sitting in front of the gun.

God will point it in his direction.
He won't have a chance for resurrection.

The Devil's power will fade if we turn our backs.
And laugh at all of his attacks.

He won't be able to feed,
on our hate or our greed.

He will be castrated. He will lose all his powers.
We will be stronger than the two towers.

He won't be able to combat our love.
So give everyone a giant hug.

Show everyone that they are your buddies.
Give them a smile that's bright and sunny.

Open your heart and sharpen your mind.
Make sure that you're not someone left behind.

It won't be nice to share the same fate,
as the Devil whose time is too late.

Barry Geistlinger

INFINITE POWER

God is a being of infinite power.
He's getting stronger every hour.

He needs our love to get the job done.
That is why he gave us his son.

We had to be saved. We're not meant to be evil.
Our lives were made for something unreal.

Our backs were made not to be broken.
Our minds were made to be more open.

Our hearts were made to love all things living.
To cherish all life that God is giving.

The animals and insects aren't to be eaten.
They have souls that must go on living.

They all have the right to try and exist.
They are so cute, they're hard to resist.

Look in your eyes and you'll see their passion.
They don't need things made just for fashion.

Their lives are simple and more complete.
All they care about is something to eat.

You must respect them like they were your own.
They've always been here to make Earth their home.

They are here to complete the cycle of life.
You should not hurt them cause they give you life.

<u>INFINITE WISDOM</u>

Try asking God for infinite wisdom.
He will give you the knowledge of heaven.

If you don't try you'll never find out.
There is a way to shed all of your doubts.

You will have knowledge to release your anger.
It only was needed to keep you from danger.

Some people are evil. Their hearts don't know why.
They would rather stick you in the eye.

Their hearts became callused because they were hurt.
All of God's love, they did desert.

They don't pray to him. They don't give him love.
They are so lost they think money is love.

They feed their egos, like they are some gods.
They neglect their children just like they are clods.

You don't have to portray some richly image.
You just have to show God you have courage.

Your time here on Earth has come to an end.
So go tell your mother. Go tell your friends.

There is a book that is here to teach us.
The meaning of life is being revealed to us.

On the last page the meaning is told.
You don't have to wait until you grow old.

THE STRENGTH TO TELL THE TRUTH

Don't go on lying straight to your self.
You need more than money to stay in health.

You are made from more than skin and bones.
God put inside you a love that is reborn.

When you accept God into your life.
You are not tied to do things that cause strife.

You feel love inside you growing and growing.
It comes with the knowledge that you will know.

God can then give you his blessings.
He'll give you answers so you won't keep guessing.

He will light the way to make a safe path.
You don't have to do all of the math.

His love is endless. He doesn't discriminate.
You don't have to be the captain or first mate.

He answers the poor. He answers the rich.
He answers the guys digging the ditch.

You have to tell yourself the truth.
God's love is there always for you.

He will do anything in his power.
As long as you ask him he will answer.

Just tell the truth about what you need.
And he'll do his best to make you succeed.

THE WILLINGNESS TO OBEY

God is calling for us to obey.
He gave us a mission to strive for each day.

We have fifty years to get the job done.
He's making sure that our life will be fun.

Don't ask him why you have been chosen.
The Devil's heart is completely frozen.

He doesn't have the ability to love.
His life is a mess. It must be removed.

He's like a thief that comes in the night.
Only to steal the part of you that's right.

He is the reason for all bad dreams.
But now he has to fight against teams.

Your love will protect you and your soul mate.
Make sure you find them before it's too late.

The children will be loved by their parents.
That is a bond that cannot be severed.

The love that is shared with friends and neighbors,
will be like a wall to block bad behaviors.

So love one another like you're the same family.
Not just on Christmas, always be happy.

The trumpets are sounding the call to duty.
We will be gaining a world filled with beauty.

Barry Geistlinger

DON'T ASK WHY

God doesn't have time to explain.
The things he asks are simple and plain.

He knows the reason why. You don't have to question.
Have faith in him to give you direction.

We are here for a purpose most divine.
The reason we're here goes back to the dawn of time.

Whatever he tells you, just go and do it.
Don't weigh the outcome. He will take you to it.

He just wants to turn our lives around.
We were going backwards not being found.

The price that we paid for being so lost.
Can't be paid back whatever the cost.

Whoever you hurt. Whatever you did.
You are forgiven. Your heart can be rid.

Of all the guilt you carried around.
It's time to make up for fooling around.

All you have to do is show some love.
Show to your friends that you are a bud.

Call up your mother and call your father.
Tell them you love them and that they matter.

You will feel better for showing your love.
You will always be their favorite cub.

BE HIS HUMBLE SERVANT

It's OK to slave for a good master.
He'll give you the strength to do it faster.

Whatever you need, will be laid down before you.
You won't have to look for a door to.

Open a way to make life be easy.
You are doing God's work by not being sleazy.

It's OK to make love when you are of age.
The love that you make will keep you engaged.

It's hard for the Devil to be around love.
He cannot get in. He can't push and shove.

Express your feelings with some kind words.
When you're with your love, you'll always be heard.

They just have to be part of your heart.
They understand because they are smart.

Don't turn away if you see tears.
Just wipe away all of your fears.

It doesn't make sense to doubt your loved one.
They care more than anyone.

When hearts are combined they triple in strength.
You have the power to go to great lengths.

You have the stamina. You have the wisdom.
To build a world that's full of freedom.

Barry Geistlinger

TELL HIM YOU LOVE HIM

Tell him you love him because he is heavenly.
He is the best father to ever be.

Give him a hug like he is there.
Give him a kiss. He doesn't care.

You can be mushy. You can be nice.
He only gives you good advice.

He's not going to place judgement on you.
Telling you you're too soft in the shoe.

He doesn't care if you are pussy foot.
He will not tell you to keep your mouth shut.

So who cares if you are milk toast?
You are just showing your love the most.

You can be tough and still be crying.
Let your emotions not being dying.

Let all the love flow right through you.
Showing your feelings is not going to kill you.

You were made to appreciate love.
To let it touch you like it's a glove.

Love will always find a way.
To fulfill the dreams you have today.

There's no mountain too high, or valley too low.
There is no distance too far for you to go.

TELL HIM WHAT YOU APPRECIATE

Whatever you love, tell him above.
He needs to know that which you love.

Tell him if you love the moon and the stars, and even the fishes.
We like all that wiggles, even in ditches.

We like all the bugs even if they're not cute.
They clean the world up that we pollute.

If we didn't have them, we'd be knee deep in crap.
There would be such a smell that we would not lap.

Even the plants are cleaning up.
Cause we produce tons of slop.

The birds take the mess out of our yard.
They use all the twigs the trees discard.

All the animals are here for a reason.
You cannot accuse them of treason.

Think of the air that you are breathing.
It is no accident that it is refreshing.

Even the seasons give us variety.
The snow and the rain console humanity.

Although the sun isn't for us to be look at.
It lights up the day making trees fun to stare at.

So the next time you start taking life for granted.
Think of how long it took God to plan it.

Barry Geistlinger

HAVE FAITH IN HIM

Have faith in him. He won't disappoint you.
He is there to give the best to you.

All good things are in his power.
He can give life to a dead flower.

With just one touch he can restore it.
He is so strong so don't ignore it.

He is like the best bodyguard.
There's nothing to fear because he hits hard.

He will look out forever for you.
Always on guard just to protect you.

Your best interest is on his mind.
He doesn't want to leave you behind.

He gives us the knowledge we need.
To paralyze the Devil so we can leave.

The new earth is better than our minds can fathom.
It's more beautiful than even heaven.

It is so rich in its abundance.
There is no smog hanging above it.

The trees are much greener than any we've seen.
All of the animals are filling the scene.

The water is so blue it is crystal clear.
It is a place devoid of tears.

DON'T DOUBT HIS LOVE

He is in love with every one of us.
His puppy dog eyes look upon us.

His love doesn't come with any conditions.
He just wants to grant all our wishes.

He hurts inside when we are lost.
He is more like a father, not like a boss.

He has more than a stake in us.
He's not getting paid for him to love us.

He does everything out of his goodness.
He is not trying to create some business.

He thinks of us all day long.
He is the artist and we are his song.

He considers us his whole life's work.
We should be grateful he's not a jerk.

He didn't have to sacrifice.
He could of left us to our own devices.

We owe him a debt of gratitude.
He doesn't deserve all of this attitude.

Our egos are wallowed up in vanity.
We should focus more on humanity.

We should take time to be more human.
After all, his love has been proven.

Barry Geistlinger

DON'T DOUBT HIS POWER

God is using, for us all his power.
He's bringing the Devil his final hour.

He's giving us life that we can be proud of.
He's giving us a world free of mischief.

It's full of plants and animals.
His creation will be like a festival.

He's giving us a home where we can party.
It's filled with love and it is heartier.

We don't have to fight for a piece of land.
We don't need a house close to the sand.

We'll be made of light and free of want.
We have the whole universe for us to jaunt.

We won't be held back by mortal restraints.
We will be free of any complaints.

We will have forever to discover each other.
You will not have to leave any brother.

All will be there, all aunts and uncles.
All your grandparents will be free of carbuncles.

No diseases will even come near us.
Only nice breezes appear before us.

The new earth is filled with enormous love.
God filled it up with all of his blood.

WE DON'T FORGET/
(the meaning of life)

We don't forget the reason God made us.
He needed someone to illustrate his.

We are his vision of peace for the future.
We are something for him to nurture.

He needs someone to give all his love.
He is a being feeding on hugs.

He needs something to put all his love in.
We are his choice apart from heaven.

He's like a sponge soaking in love.
His heart needs for us to love.

His mind doesn't know any evil.
We are his babies to be revealed.

His whole life mission has been to receive us.
Into his arms he wants to see us.

He wants to live with us forever.
He wants to enjoy all of us together.

He wants to be the MC of the party.
He wants us all to see how he's happy.

He wishes he could show everyone now.
Just how much we make him feel proud.

He thinks we all did a good job.
Keeping the Devil inside that glob.

0-595-34093-8

Made in the USA
Lexington, KY
29 November 2011